THE GREAT
WONDER

ODYSSEY

This book is dedicated to Doris, Peggy, Margeurite and RB. —A.H.

Copyright © 1996 Trudy Corporation, 353 Main Avenue, Norwalk, CT 06851,
and the Smithsonian Institution, Washington, DC 20560

Soundprints is a division of Trudy Corporation, Norwalk, Connecticut.

Book design: Alleycat Design Inc. New York, NY

First Edition
10 9   8   7   6   5   4   2   1
Printed in Hong Kong

Library of Congress Cataloging-in-Publication Data

Howard, Annabelle.
    The great wonder : The building of the Great Pyramid / by Annabelle Howard ;
illustrated by Stephen Wells.
        p.   cm.

    Summary: While on a field trip to Smithsonian's Museum of Natural History, Kevin
imagines himself taking part in the final stage of the construction of the Great Pyramid near
the Egyptian town of Giza more than 4000 years ago.

    ISBN 1-56899-350-1 (hardcover). —ISBN 1-56899-351-X (pbk.)
    [1. Pyramids—Egypt—Fiction. 2. Egypt—Antiquities—Fiction. 3. School field trips—
Fiction.] I. Wells, Stephen, ill. II. Title.
PZ7. H83235Gr   1996
[Fic]—dc20
                                                96-11361
                                                    CIP
                                                    AC

THE GREAT WONDER

Written by Annabelle Howard
Illustrated by Stephen Wells

Soundprints
Where Children Discover...

It is cool and dark in the theater at the Smithsonian's National Museum of Natural History exhibit on Western Civilization. Kevin and his friends collapse gratefully onto the carpeted step benches.

"It's so hot outside, I thought I was going to melt!" Lucy moans.

"Shhh!" Tomas hushes his friends. "The movie's starting."

"What's it about?" Emma asks.

"Pyramids and mummies and pharaohs!" Kevin says enthusiastically.

"Pyramids are so boring!" Tomas complains.

"How can you say that?" Kevin is amazed. "The pyramids were huge—almost five hundred feet tall! It took thousands of men twenty years just to build *one* of them."

"Exactly what I mean," Tomas sighs. He thinks fast food isn't fast enough.

As the movie lights up the screen, Kevin leans forward. The narrator describes life in Ancient Egypt on the banks of the Nile River and the momentous task of building the pyramids.

"Can you believe it?" Kevin whispers to Emma. "Every one of the stones had to be cut by hand and pulled all the way from the quarry!"

"I know," Emma replies, "And most of them weighed more than a car. How do you think they did it?"

"I don't know. I get tired just carrying my backpack!"

"Shhh!" Lucy signals to Kevin and Emma from the row in front of them. She is already involved in the movie.

Emma giggles and Kevin tries to silence her with a nudge of his elbow. But his elbow smacks against a cold, stone wall!

"Ow!" Rubbing his elbow, Kevin scans his new surroundings. He is not in the theater anymore.

What is this place? he wonders, squinting into the darkness. He is sitting in a huge stone box. His legs, stretched out in front of him, don't even reach one third of the way across the smooth, gray bottom.

This is creepy! This box looks like a coffin. If it is, it was meant for someone bigger than me!

He jumps up, ready to climb out. A draft breezes by his legs. Looking down, he screams in surprise. He is wearing nothing but a short, white skirt!

Tomas, Emma, and Lucy sure would get a laugh out of this! He ducks down, blushing. *I guess I could stay here for now!*

Peering over the box's edge, Kevin's eyes adjust to the light. He is in a large, empty room. A dim torch casts shadows on walls of smooth stone.

Is this a castle? Or a dungeon? he wonders. *Wait a minute . . .* he thinks back to the movie at the museum and its description of the Great Pyramid.

"I'm in the Great Pyramid! And this must be King Khufu's chamber," Kevin blurts out excitedly, looking at the high ceilings and walls, "deep inside the pyramid!"

Then Kevin realizes where he is sitting. "Since this pyramid is a tomb for King Khufu," he stutters, "then this must be his coffin—a sarcophagus for the dead pharaoh!" He climbs out of the box as fast as he can!

It's time to do some exploring! Kevin feels like an archeologist, ready for adventure. This is better than any museum. He is experiencing history in the making.

Heading toward the doorway, Kevin stops in his tracks. He hears an echo of footsteps and a murmur of voices in the distance. They are growing louder and closer. And the voices don't sound friendly!

"I thought I heard someone in the King's Chamber," booms a man's voice.

"There shouldn't be!" answers another. "I thought we were the last workers to leave the pyramid. The rest of the men are all outside."

Kevin thinks fast—he could pretend to be a worker. But how would he explain why he wasn't outside helping? Quickly, Kevin crouches behind the sarcophagus to hide.

Suddenly, the room is brighter from the light of a torch. Two burly men loom in the doorway.

"I'll look in the sarcophagus. You check the air shafts," one of them orders.

Kevin's heart is beating fast now. One of the men steps closer! Kevin leaps out from behind the sarcophagus and darts past the startled men. He runs through the entranceway into the room in front of the King's Chamber, the antechamber.

This room is as empty and plain as the first, but leads to another doorway. Kevin shuffles through the low passageway. The light is dim and he doesn't see the floor slope ahead of him. He tumbles forward, landing on the hard stone of the Grand Gallery.

The men are quickly catching up to him. Kevin finds a hiding place behind a large block of stone and squeezes in.

When the men reach the Grand Gallery, they race right past him.

"I didn't see him!" one yells in frustration.

"We've lost him!" the other agrees.

Kevin breathes a sigh of relief. *This is some game of hide and seek!*

"We can't waste any more time," says one man. "They need us to haul the capstone. Let's go."

Kevin waits until the men leave the gallery, then steps out.

The capstone! They must still be building the pyramid. I've got to see this!

Kevin follows the workers out of the gallery. He is careful to go unnoticed as they crawl through the low, sloping passages by torch light—down and then up again.

As they climb upward, Kevin runs his hands along the flat, smooth walls. *The workers must have polished these giant stones! They fit so closely together!* he thinks. *Without any modern tools, too—just chisels, and saws, and sand!* Kevin is definitely impressed. *It must take weeks to finish one stone!*

The journey out of the pyramid seems to take forever. Kevin is getting impatient. But when he feels a blast of warm air and sees a square of light up ahead, he knows they are almost to the hot desert outside.

At the end of the passage, the men disappear into the daylight. Kevin waits until he is sure they are gone and steps out into the blazing Egyptian sunlight.

He is standing at the entrance to the pyramid, about fifty-five feet above the ground. The sun has been beating against the limestone steps all morning and they feel like fire against Kevin's bare feet. He shifts from one foot to the other as he looks out over the desert.

Long reed boats glide across the Nile, heavy with limestone blocks from the quarry at Tura, about three or four miles away. Small huts made of mud and rubble surround the base of the pyramid. Lots of workers bustle back and forth. Dressed like the other workers, Kevin will blend right in with the busy crowd.

He starts his long climb down the side of
the pyramid. Each step is even taller than him!
When he reaches the bottom he is hot, and
very, very thirsty.

Kevin finds a bucket and takes a long drink of water. Then he sees a shadow of someone behind him. He turns. It is one of the workers who chased him inside the pyramid!

"I was just . . ." Kevin stammers.

"It's not break time yet," the man says. He doesn't recognize Kevin from before. Instead, he hands Kevin a wooden mallet and a chisel.

He and Kevin join a team of workers carving a group of casing blocks, the stones that will cover the pyramid structure and give it its smooth finish. Kevin watches the man whack the chisel with the mallet and does the same to his block of stone. One worker scratches the team's name on each block. When no one else is looking, Kevin scratches a *K* on his stone.

The men stop to rest, and Kevin decides to slip away and explore. He wanders to the east side of the giant pyramid, which is shaded by the sun making it a bit cooler. Above, Kevin sees the capstone—a pointed stone covered in gold—near the end of the supply ramp.

The ramp runs from the ground all the way to the top of the pyramid. It is nearly a mile long and is almost as impressive as the pyramid itself!

There is no elevator here! Kevin thinks. *If I want to see the capstone, I'll have to use the ramp!*

He sprints to the ramp's base, far from the pyramid. When he arrives, he is already out of breath and the desert heat burns his skin. *I can't believe they built this just to transport supplies!* he thinks.

He starts his climb. He has a long way to catch up with the capstone!

After a half hour of running up the ramp, Kevin finally reaches the workers. They are pulling and tugging the massive stone. The capstone sits heavily on a wooden sled, as if challenging the men to move it further. Several men struggle, trying to heave it from below, rolling it over huge logs. Others pull tightly from above on a rope tied to the sled's base.

Kevin thought he was exhausted, but these men must be even more tired than him! They have been dragging the capstone for days! Kevin is eager to give it a try.

Suddenly, a shout rings out. Two men tumble to the ground and drop a giant log. It rolls right toward Kevin! Panicked, Kevin looks for an escape, but he has nowhere to run!

A worker leaps in front of Kevin, carrying a long lever. He wedges one end into the soft ramp and diverts the oncoming log. The log flies off the side of the ramp and falls to the ground at the pyramid's base.

"That could have been me!" Kevin watches the log fall over the edge. "Thanks," he squeaks to the other worker.

When the capstone reaches the end of the ramp, it can no longer be pulled. It must be pushed from below. Kevin sees the workers struggling and offers to help them. Together, they lean all of their weight against the levers, and the sled lurches forward. More workers push their levers into the new space behind the sled, and the capstone creeps upward.

At the top of the pyramid, the workers use more logs to lift the capstone from its sled and carefully slide it onto a wooden frame.

As the hours pass, an enormous crowd gathers below. They all wait breathlessly as Kevin's crew slides the golden peak onto the pyramid.

Craftsmen check to make sure that the stone is positioned and then they pull out the wooden frame. As the capstone slides into place, a cloud of white dust rises into the sky, mingling with the triumphant roar of the crowd below. They have worked many years toward this big event.

The sun sinks in the West and its strong rays shine off the glistening capstone. The men start down the ramp. It is the end of a long day. Tomorrow, they will start placing the casing stones.

Kevin lingers behind. He feels very small as he stands alone, four hundred and eighty-one feet above the ancient Egyptian world. *This is just like being at the top of the Washington Monument,* realizes Kevin. *And these pyramids were built so long ago. What a great wonder this is!*

Kevin rubs his eyes as he looks at the view below. They sting from the dust, sweat and sun.

As Kevin rubs his eyes, someone tugs his arm.

He opens his eyes and sees the familiar museum theater. Tomas is pulling on his sleeve.

"Come on!" he says. "It's time to go home. We can't sit in this theater all day!"

Kevin jumps up, excited to tell his friends about his adventure. But Tomas, Emma, and Lucy are already out the exit door. On second thought, Kevin decides to keep his adventure to himself —for now.

Outside, Kevin catches up to them. The monuments around Washington don't seem as impressive as they did before Kevin saw the Great Pyramid.

"It's as hot as the desert out here!" Lucy remarks.

"Not really," answers Kevin. "It's a *lot* hotter in the desert!" Before Lucy can respond, he adds, "At least that's what I've heard."

ABOUT THE GREAT PYRAMID

The Great Pyramid, considered one of the Seven Wonders of the World, is the largest stone building ever built. There is enough stone in it to build a low wall once around the earth. It stands as tall as a 40-story building.

The Great Pyramid was built as a tomb for King Khufu, a pharaoh, who was buried in the King's Chamber, within the pyramid, around the year 2,566 B.C. When first built, the Great Pyramid stood at 481 feet, but the top was later stripped away. It stands in Egypt along the Nile River, near the town of Giza. Two other pyramids and the Great Sphinx stand close to the Great Pyramid. The other two pyramids were built for Khufu's son, Khafre, and his grandson, Menkure. Smaller pyramids are also located nearby and are believed to have been built for other family members.

Once the pharaohs were placed in their tombs, the chambers were sealed with heavy stones. The pharaohs were buried with many valuable belongings because they believed they would need these things in their life after death. Despite the stone blocks and the maze of passageways inside each pyramid, designed to keep robbers away, a lot of the treasures were stolen from the pyramids.

Even today, with all of our modern tools and machinery, the Great Pyramid is still considered one of the most incredible engineering feats in history.

GLOSSARY

air shafts: inclined openings within the King's chamber, used for ventilation or religious purposes

casing blocks: the stones on the outside of an ancient pyramid. They were polished until shiny. The light from the sun and the stars made the casing stones shine white.

capstone: the pyramid shaped stone at the very top of a pyramid

chisel: a tool used to cut and shape stone

Grand Gallery: the tall, narrow room next to the King's Chamber. It is believed to have stored the granite plugs that were used to seal the King's Chamber after his body had been placed in the burial chamber.

King's Chamber: the burial room for the king. His body was placed in the sarcophagus, and treasures were sealed within the room.

King Khufu: the king for whom the Great Pyramid was built

lever: a rigid bar used to exert a pressure or sustain a weight at one end by the application of force at the other end

limestone: a rock that is formed from the collection of organic remains, such as shells and coral; the primary stone used for the building of the Great Pyramid

mallet: a hammer-like tool, usually with a large barrel-shaped head, used for driving another tool or for striking a surface without damaging it

Nile: the longest river in the world, which originates in central Africa. It flows north to the Mediterranean Sea, through Egypt, and past the Great Pyramid.

pharaohs: the rulers of ancient Egypt

quarry: an area used for excavating stone. For the building of the Great Pyramid, the quarry was for obtaining and preparing the limestone. The location of the pyramid, at the time of its construction, was also a quarry that supplied some of the core blocks of the pyramid.

Queen's Chamber: a room in the pyramid, below the King's Chamber, that was never completed

sarcophagus: a large, stone, rectangular coffin. A wooden coffin containing the pharaoh's body was placed inside the sarcophagus.

Tura: the location of the quarry where the workers mined and shaped the limestone